P R E F A C E

Quality management is essential for survival in today's competitive business arena. The ability to create a quality consciousness in a company is the foundation on which quality improvement must be built. The quotes selected for this booklet are intended to stimulate thinking about the commitment to excellence that exists in your organization.

Quality thought always preceeds quality products and services.

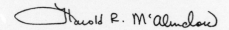

Written and Compiled by Harold R. McAlindon

Calligraphy by Natalie Lombard

ISBN: 0-931089-70-0

Printed in the U.S.A.

Quality remains long after the price is forgotten.

H. Gordon Selfridge

"Good enough" is not "good enough".

The goal
of quality
is zero
defects.

CQ3

The measurement of quality is the price of non-conformance. "Do it right the first time."

Quality
*is never an accident; it is
always the result of high
intention, sincere effort,
intelligent direction and
skillful execution; it
represents the wise
choice of many
alternatives.*

Will A. Foster

Computers cannot tell you about the quality of your product...the human eye and human experience is the one thing that can make quality better... or poorer.

Stanley Marcus

Few people go to work intending to perform poorly. Managers must show them how to pursue excellence.

A company's commitment to quality makes people proud to work there.

There is always a better way...your challenge is to find it.

Nothing attracts customers like quality.

CQ10

Quality standards are contagious... spread them throughout the organization.

Quality is a hands-on proposition.

Tom Peters

Quality
marks the search for
an ideal after
necessity has been
satisfied and mere
usefulness achieved.

Will A. Foster

CQ13

Quality is defined as a conformance to requirements not as a goodness.

Quality improvement is built on getting everyone to "do it right the first time".

CQ15

Anything that reduces quality can be prevented.

It's amazing how close to perfection you can get if... you're willing to try.

CQ17

When quality doesn't improve it usually means you're not dedicated enough.

Quality goes up when management has high expectations for their staff.

Commitment to quality can be a great rallying force.

CQ20

If
quality
is sacrificed
society is
not truly
served.

H. T. Garvey

Excellence implies more than competence... it implies a striving for the highest possible standards.

*here*
*is a huge difference
between "the best money
can buy" and "the best
value for the dollar".
Knowing which is most
important to the
customer is crucial.*

The guarantee of continuity is quality.

Capt. Edward Rickenbacker

There is only one way to have a successful company. . .to have a lot of happy, satisfied customers.

If <u>you</u> don't keep "doing it better". . .your competition will.

CQ26

When you're out of quality you're out of business.

The system for creating quality is preventing not appraisal.

Quality
only happens
when you care
enough to do
your best.

CQ29

Customers are loyal to quality not the company.

CQ30

Quality
is an eternal
struggle.

Quality
is not a department
responsibility.
Quality is everyone
and everything
within an
organization.

CQ32

Real
quality is
free.

Phil Crosby

Quality begets quality in everything.

Quality assurance must be supported by quality improvement.

*Q*uality
*must be active
rather than
re-active.*

Quality
*is a dynamic
rather than a
static process.*

The difference in failure and success is doing a thing nearly right and doing a thing exactly right.

Quality is never having to say you're sorry.

Our quality "PERFORMANCE" has not kept pace with our quality "KNOWLEDGE".

CQ40

The difference between ordinary and extraordinary is that little extra.

*If better
is possible,
good is not
enough.*

Don't try to "sell what you have"...rather "have what people need and value".

CQ43

*Every job
is a self-portrait
of the person who did
it. Autograph
your work with
excellence.*

Quality
is essentially
attention
to detail.

*There
is only one rule of
business and that is:
Make the best quality
at the lowest cost
possible.*

Henry Ford

It is quality rather than quantity that matters.

Seneca

Quality
is meeting our customers' requirements at all times and striving to exceed them whenever possible.

CQ48

It is just the little difference between the good and the best that makes the difference between the artist and the artisan. It is just the little touches after the average man would quit that make the master's fame.

Orison Swett Marden

Quality products and services will never exceed that quality of the management team.

Quality must not only exist...it must be perceived by the customer.

CQ51

Quality products and quality service begin with quality thinking.

Quality
that is not measured
is a slogan not a
system.

CQ53

Quality requires tenacity of purpose.

Quality
is improved not only
by those <u>achieving</u>
excellence...but also
by those who are
trying.

CQ55

Quality
means "adherence
to standards".

Phil Crosby

Quality is not a department.... It is an organization wide commitment.

CQ57

Quality criteria must
exist for
every function.

CQ58

Quality improvement is a never ending process.

To produce quality you must have a "system" to improve it.

It takes courageous leadership to admit that "we must improve our quality."

CQ61

Quality levels must not only be attained, but maintained, and improved.

*Americans
still care
about quality. The
country is full of
intelligent, courageous
people who
would change if they
only knew how.*

W. Edwards Deming

Everyone must be <u>expected</u> to contribute ideas to improve quality.

*S*et
*quality
improvement
goals.*

CQ65

Your work is you. Don't let you down.

If you don't believe in quality. . .you'll never produce it.

*commitment
to quality
must start at the
top.*

Most quality problems exist because we don't take the issue seriously enough.

$\mathcal{Y}$ou must know the cost of "poor quality".

Quality products and services evolve from quality work environments.

Sam L. Moore

Get rid of anyone who thinks quality standards "are a pain in the neck".

Every employee must know their contribution to quality.

Much good work is lost for the lack of a little more.

E. H. Harriman

Just make up your mind at the very outset that your work is going to stand for quality. . .that you are going to stamp a superior quality upon everything that goes out of your hands, that whatever you do shall bear the hall-mark of excellence.

Orison Swett Marden

"The thoughts expressed in this booklet were intended to stimulate and challenge you. Share them with others. Talk about them. Reflect on them. Use them. Put them into action."

Good Luck,

[signature: Mac Anderson]

President
Great Quotations Inc.

A B O U T   T H E   A U T H O R

Harold R. McAlindon, president of the Innovation Institute, is one of the nation's most respected consultants and management personalities. He is the author of "Getting the Most Out of Your Job and Your Organization," is featured on the cover of "Creative Innovators" and has published over 75 articles. His books by Great Quotations include: <u>Think</u>, <u>Commitment to Quality</u>, <u>Customer Care</u>, <u>What Motivates People</u> and <u>Management Magic</u>.

He has won many national awards and specializes in consulting with companies on how to develop and maintain high levels of quality, customer service and innovation. He has also been selected as one of the top management speakers in America by the International Platform Association, The Presidents Association and The World Future Society.

If you would like to inquire about utilizing Harold as a consultant or having him speak to your group, please call us and we'll be happy to send you more information. Call toll free 1-800-621-1432 or (312) 953-1222.

Other Great Quotations Books :

- Best of Success
- Business Quotes
- Commitment to Excellence
- Commitment to Quality
- Customer Care
- Golf Quotes
- Great Quotes/Great Leaders
- Great Quotes/Great Women
- Management Magic
- Motivational Quotes
- Opportunity Selling
- Think
- What Motivates People
- Winning Words

GREAT QUOTATIONS, INC.
919 SPRINGER DRIVE • LOMBARD, IL 60148-6416

TOLL FREE: 800-621-1432 (outside Illinois)
(312) 953-1222